A CLIMATE IN CHAOS

by Neal Layton

wren
&rook

You've probably heard about climate change. At least I hope you have – because it's REALLY IMPORTANT.

It affects all of us living on Planet Earth right now, and everyone and everything that will live on our planet in the future.

Wow, that sounds pretty important!
But what exactly is it?

To understand climate change, you need to know that the climate isn't the same thing as the weather. Weather can change in just a few hours.

But climate can take many years to change – and it affects the WHOLE planet.

When the world was formed 4.5 billion years ago, the Earth's climate was very different.

At first it was crazy hot. But over the next few billion years, it began to cool. Oceans and land started to appear and life sprang into being.

Thank goodness for that!

And over this huge amount of time, our planet developed lots of different systems that allow life to flourish.

We're the first form of life!
Gradually larger life forms appeared.
There are now many millions of different life forms on our planet.
YAY!
I'm A DINOSAUR!

For example, most animals, including humans, need to breathe in order to stay alive. When we breathe, we take in an invisible gas called OXYGEN, and then we breathe out another invisible gas called CARBON DIOXIDE.

Plants need to do something a bit like breathing to stay alive too. But they do it the other way around, taking in carbon dioxide and releasing oxygen.

High above the surface of Planet Earth is a layer of what scientists call greenhouse gases. Carbon dioxide is a type of greenhouse gas. Any carbon dioxide that isn't taken in by plants travels up into the sky to join the other greenhouse gases. These gases help keep our planet warm, like an invisible duvet. They're important, because we humans need warmth to live.

greenhouse gases

Plants in the ocean also take in carbon dioxide and release oxygen. Actually, most of our oxygen comes from the oceans.

In fact, you could think of Earth like a giant spaceship, whizzing through space around the Sun and providing us with everything we need to survive: WARMTH and OXYGEN along with FOOD and WATER.

When you stop to think about it, Planet Earth has been very good to us.

Wow!

Space is VERY cold and there is no oxygen, no food and no water.

VROOM!

But 200 years ago, things began to change.
Humans started making machines powered by burning things.

This made life easier for lots of people. But it had other effects too.

Do you remember those greenhouse gases like carbon dioxide? When anything gets burned, it makes MORE of those gases. So every time we burn something, perhaps in a petrol engine or a coal-fired power station, we release more gases into the air.

Another type of greenhouse gas is methane. We release it when we farm cows and put rubbish in landfills.

And we're not just making more greenhouse gases. We're also chopping down huge areas of forest. So there are a lot fewer plants and trees to take in the carbon dioxide from the air.

All this is building a thicker layer of greenhouse gases, a bigger duvet, and it's warming up our planet. About 70 years ago, scientists began to notice that our planet was getting hotter. Hotter than since records began.

Great! I like sunny days!

Well, unfortunately it's not as simple as that. Our climate getting warmer is having LOTS of different effects. This is what we call climate change.

Firstly long-term weather is changing, causing...

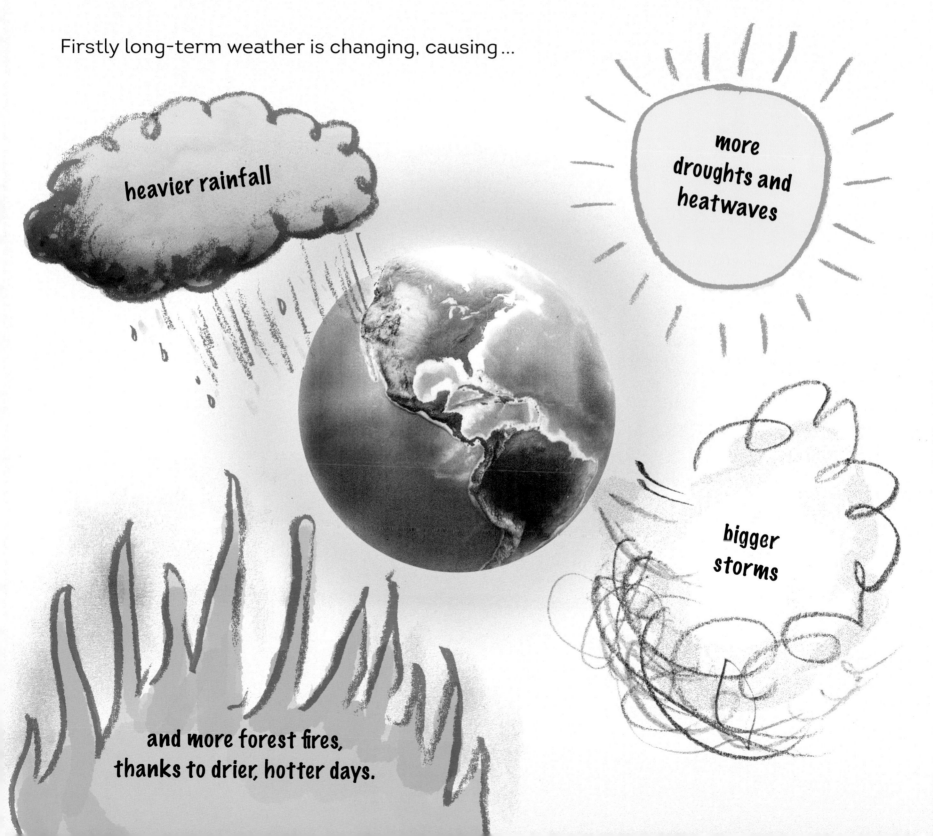

heavier rainfall

more droughts and heatwaves

bigger storms

and more forest fires, thanks to drier, hotter days.

Higher temperatures and changed weather systems are affecting animals' habitats too.

Polar bears hunt for seals on the icy platform of the Arctic sea. Climate change is melting it.

Elephants need to drink lots of fresh water each day, but hotter, drier weather is making it much more difficult for them to find it.

Adélie penguins feed on tiny krill which live under the Antarctic ice. Less ice and warmer waters mean fewer krill for the penguins to eat.

Insects like butterflies and bumblebees are also struggling. Insects are really important because bigger animals like lizards, birds and frogs eat them as food.

Giant pandas only eat bamboo. But climate change is causing less bamboo to grow in the pandas' natural habitat, leaving them hungry.

A healthy coral reef should be full of colour and life, but because the ocean is becoming too warm, corals are starting to look like this. It's called coral bleaching.

All over the world, animals from very small insects to big mammals are facing problems because climate change is transforming their habitats, making it harder for them to find food, water and shelter.

This isn't right. I like
our planet the way it is.

I'm glad you said that.

To stop our planet overheating, we need to stop creating greenhouse gases.

Transportation

Cars, lorries, ships and planes release greenhouse gases when they burn fuel. We need people to travel by train and bus more. Cycling or walking is even better!

Things

Factories release carbon dioxide when making things for us to buy. So if we think carefully and buy only things we really need, it will help reduce the amount of greenhouse gases.

Food

Eating plants rather than meat reduces the amount of methane in the air. And by buying food grown locally, or even growing our own, we can avoid burning fuel to transport food, which is much better for the planet.

Energy

Most of the energy we use to power our homes comes from burning greenhouse gases. If we waste less energy in our homes, we won't have to produce so many harmful gases.

Waste

Throwing unwanted things into our rubbish bins creates greenhouse gases when they are buried in landfill or burned. Less waste means fewer greenhouse gases.

Reduce, reuse, recycle!

Growing

All plants take in carbon dioxide, helping us to solve the climate-change problem. So we need to grow more plants and trees rather than chopping down forests. And growing more forests will give lots of animals somewhere to live!

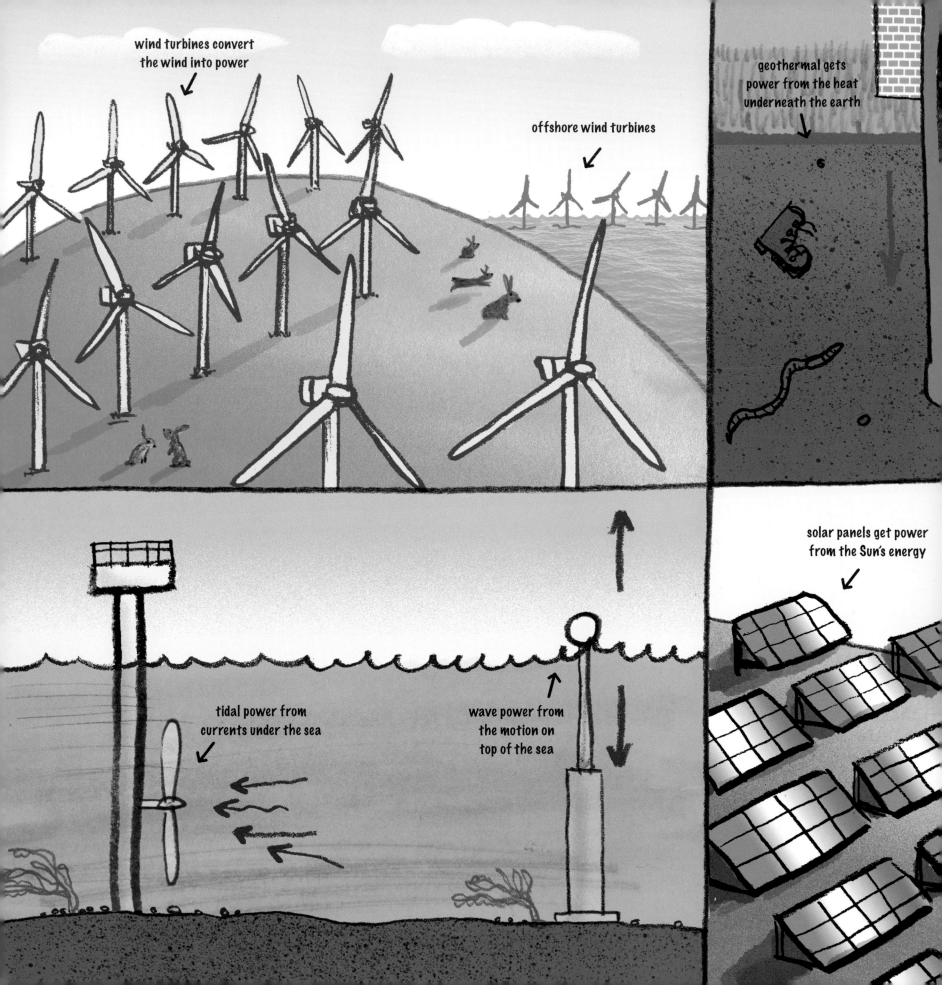

But to really make a difference and stop climate change, we need to think bigger.

Most greenhouse gases are released by burning coal, oil or gas in power stations.

We need to switch to renewable energy sources like WIND, TIDAL, GEOTHERMAL and SOLAR power.

Ultimately, we need to think about how us humans can treat the planet better by changing how we live. After all, we depend upon it for everything!

Scientists call this sustainable living. Here's a picture of what a sustainable home of the future might look like.

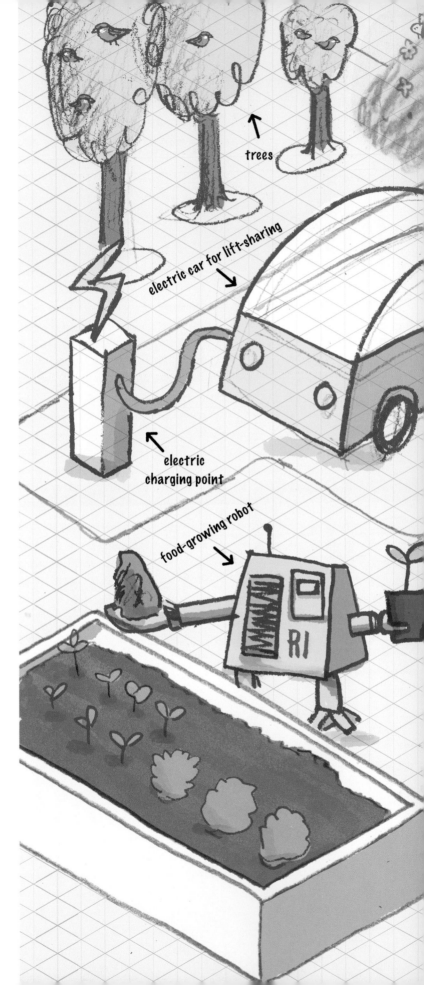

trees

electric car for lift-sharing

electric charging point

food-growing robot

RI

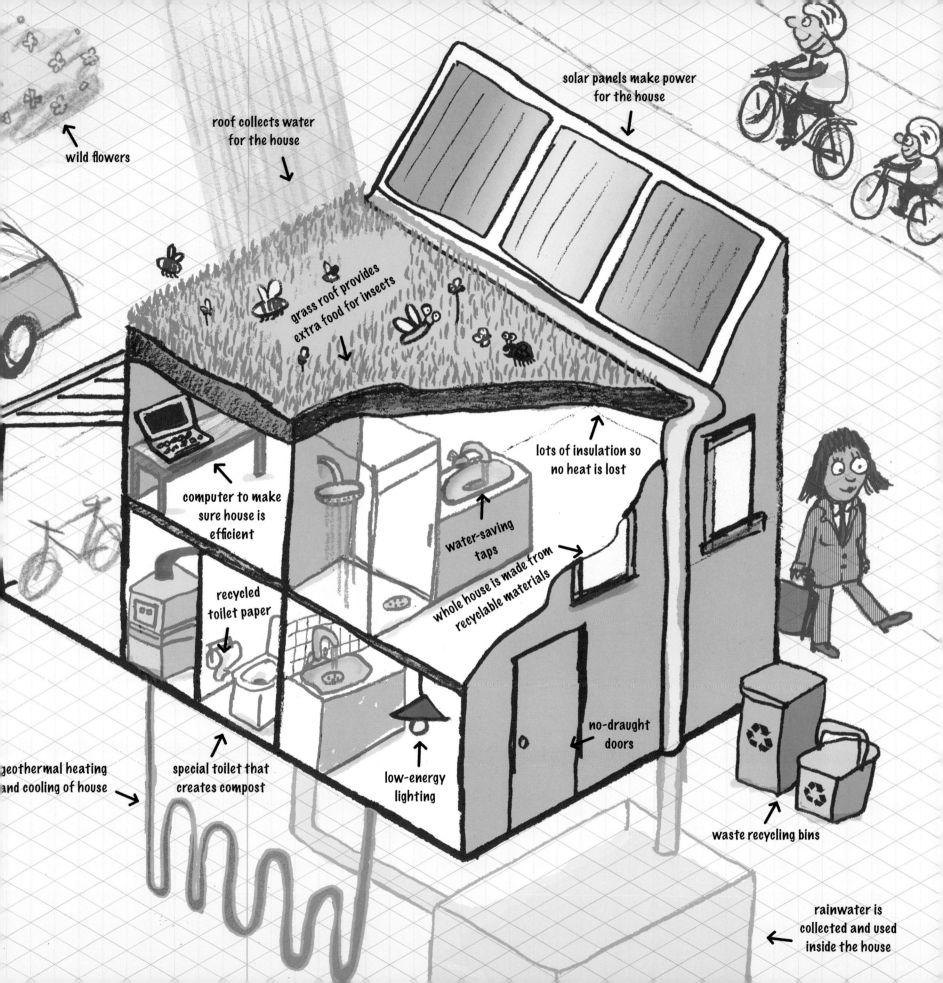

Of course, people all around the world have already started to make big, positive changes.

These ideas look much better!

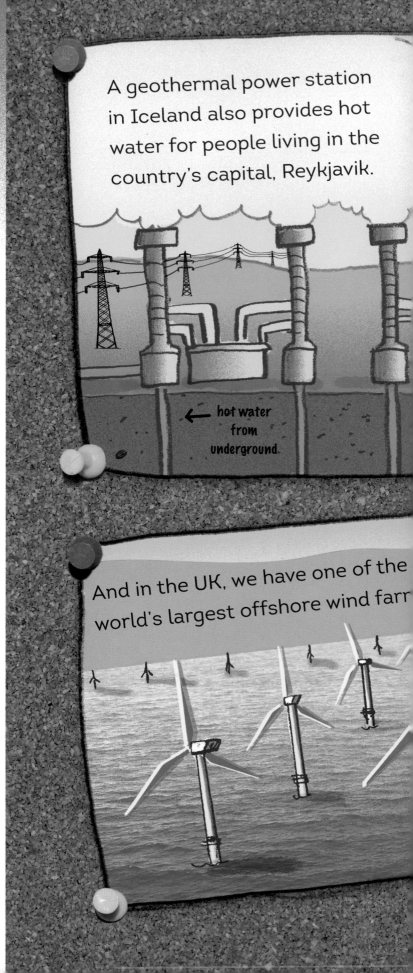

A geothermal power station in Iceland also provides hot water for people living in the country's capital, Reykjavik.

← hot water from underground

And in the UK, we have one of the world's largest offshore wind farm

Lots of countries are planting new forests. In China, just one charity has planted 24 million trees!

Scientists and engineers are also looking at how to replace fuel-burning cars and planes with alternatives like electric cars and even electric flying taxis for short journeys.

cleaner air

electric air taxi

electric ride-share taxi

One thing most scientists agree on is that we need to act soon, because if we don't, we might not be able to stop climate change.

It's a big problem that affects everyone across the planet in different ways. There are more than 7.7 billion people living on Earth right now. If we all did a little bit to help, it would add up to a lot.

Like me and my big brother?

Exactly!

HELP OUR PLANET

Hey folks!

Have you heard about climate change?
It's **REALLY IMPORTANT**.

It affects all of us living on Planet Earth right now,
and everyone and everything that will live on our
planet in the future.

This is what we need to do …

Here's how you can help

There are lots of practical ways you can make a difference!

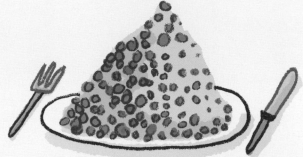

1 Reduce, reuse and repair. Instead of buying new things, mend and reuse your old things.

2 Walk or cycle as much as possible. And if your family does need to travel in a conventional car, try to fill up all the seats by offering lifts to other people.

3 Turn off your televisions, phone chargers and other electrical appliances when you aren't using them. Leaving them on standby uses almost as much power as when they're fully switched on!

4 Eat your greens rather than lots of meat. You don't need to cut out meat completely – how about leaving meat out of your meals for one or two days each week?

5 Keep learning about climate change and talk to your family and friends about it. If everyone understands what is happening, we can work together to find solutions.

And you know, it's not just grown-ups who have BIG ideas...

GRETA THUNBERG was just 15 when, instead of going to school, she first sat outside the Swedish Parliament to protest inaction over climate change. Now, her weekly #schoolstrike4climate is a global movement that has inspired millions of kids and grown-ups.

In 2017, nine-year-old **RIDHIMA PANDEY** sued the Indian government, asking judges to make sure that her country's politicians started doing more to help the environment.

SAHIL DOSHI is a young scientist who, at the age of 14, invented the PolluCell. It's a battery powered by recycled carbon dioxide and other waste materials, helping to tackle pollution!

So, can you think of a big idea to help save the planet?

GLOSSARY

Carbon dioxide — A gas released by the burning of coal, natural gas, oil and wood that traps heat in the atmosphere.

Climate — The average pattern of weather over a long period of time. Climate isn't weather – weather changes daily.

Habitat — The home of an animal or a plant.

Fossil fuels — Coal, oil and natural gas, which come from the breakdown of ancient plants and animals over millions of years.

Many thanks to Dr James Dyke of University of Exeter for technical assistance writing the book, and to Dr Huw Lewis Jones of Falmouth University for the use of photographic images from his polar expeditions.

This book is dedicated to eco-warriors everywhere, young and old.

First published in Great Britain in 2020 by Wren & Rook

HB ISBN: 978 1 5263 6230 8
PB ISBN: 978 1 5263 6231 5
E-book ISBN: 978 1 5263 6232 2
10 9 8 7 6 5 4 3 2 1

Wren & Rook
An imprint of Hachette Children's Group
Part of Hodder & Stoughton
Carmelite House, 50 Victoria Embankment, London EC4Y 0DZ

An Hachette UK Company
www.hachette.co.uk
www.hachettechildrens.co.uk

Publishing Director: Debbie Foy
Managing Editor: Liza Miller
Creative Director: Sophie Stericker

Printed in China

Picture acknowledgements: The publisher would like to thank the following for permission to reproduce their pictures: front cover Chuenmanuse / Shutterstock.com; p. 13 © David Jones; p. 15 Globcal International; pp. 18-19 Dr Huw Lewis Jones; p. 29 Lisa Padilla / Flickr.com.